WHAT ARE TUESDAYS LIKE?

Victor Bumbalo

BROADWAY PLAY PUBLISHING INC
224 E 62nd St, NY, NY 10065
www.broadwayplaypub.com
info@broadwayplaypub.com

WHAT ARE TUESDAYS LIKE?
© Copyright 2010 by Victor Bumbalo

First printing: June 2010
I S B N: 978-0-88145-418-5

Book design: Marie Donovan
Typographic controls: Adobe Indesign
Typeface: Palatino
Printed and bound in the U S A

CHARACTERS & SETTING

HOWARD, *late forties*
JEFF, *thirties*
SCOTT, *late twenties*
GENE, *thirties*
DENISE, *thirties*
RANDY, *late twenties*

Place: New York City. The out-patient waiting room of a hospital

Time: The early 1990s

The author wishes to thank the following people for their inspiration, talent, and help: Jeremy Lawrence, Ed Herendeen, Frank Gagliano, Dan Lauria, Ricahrd Sachs, Michael Canter, David Milch, and Chris deBlasio.

for Robert and Tom

Scene One

(Tuesday afternoon)

(At this time every week only people with AIDS are scheduled for services. Four men are in the room. Two of the men, SCOTT and GENE, are seated close to each other. The other two, HOWARD and JEFF, sit apart from the couple and each other.)

(HOWARD is gregarious and commands authority. His chatty nature stems from a genuine interest in people. There is an inner calm to this man that people find attractive.)

(JEFF is obviously frail. Although he tries to hide it, the fear he lives with is evident.)

(SCOTT is attractive and intense. He holds on to his individuality by hiding his true nature from most people.)

(GENE likes to be in control.)

(At the moment no one is speaking. GENE has his arm around SCOTT. HOWARD is watching JEFF who is staring at a page of a magazine.)

HOWARD: Excuse me, may I ask, what is it you're reading?

JEFF: What?

HOWARD: I know it's is none of my business, but you've been staring at the same page for over thirty-five minutes. I was just curious what was so fascinating.

JEFF: (*Showing him the magazine*) It's a picture of the Grand Canyon. I was meditating on it. Trying to put myself into the picture. (*Pointing to a specific spot in the picture*) I was standing there.

HOWARD: You weren't planning to jump in?

JEFF: Why? Do I look suicidal?

HOWARD: No. I was kidding.

SCOTT: (*From the other side of the room*) Just what we need in this room—a comic.

HOWARD: Excuse me?

SCOTT: (*From the other side of the room*) Nothing.

JEFF: I don't understand. I was scheduled fifteen minutes ago for my chemotherapy, and there's no one here to give it to me. I can't be waiting around here all day.

HOWARD: It's usually not like this on Tuesdays.

SCOTT: (*From the other side of the room*) I don't want to do this.

GENE: It won't be as bad as you think.

SCOTT: How do you know?

HOWARD: (*To JEFF*) Does it work?

JEFF: What?

HOWARD: Your meditation.

JEFF: No. Maybe. I don't know. It passes the time. I can't be waiting all day for them. If they don't take me in a few minutes, I'm going to have to go.

HOWARD: You shouldn't do that.

JEFF: I'm going to have to.

HOWARD: Why don't you go back to your picture.

JEFF: I can't concentrate anymore. (*Offering* HOWARD *the magazine*) Would you like to try?

HOWARD: No, thank you.

SCOTT: (*To* JEFF) Excuse me, what's it like, the chemotherapy?

JEFF: It probably isn't as bad as you imagine.

GENE: (*To* SCOTT) See.

SCOTT: But you've lost some hair.

JEFF: Not everyone does.

GENE: (*To* SCOTT) See.

JEFF: (*To* HOWARD) What are you here for?

HOWARD: To see Louise. She's a therapist.

JEFF: Is she nice?

HOWARD: Very non-directive. But she can use some help dressing.

JEFF: I used to see Don, the other therapist.

HOWARD: Was he nice?

JEFF: Wonderful. Very humane. Had these sparkling eyes. But he flipped out.

HOWARD: I can understand.

JEFF: One day I arrived here for my appointment and he wasn't here. He disappeared. Never even gave the hospital notice. My lover, Mack, tried to track him down, but he wasn't very successful. The last thing any of his friends heard was that he was getting in his car and just going. I hope he's all right.

HOWARD: He's probably at your Grand Canyon leading those donkey tours.

JEFF: That would be great, wouldn't it?

SCOTT: (*From the other side of the room*) Or maybe he jumped in.

GENE: Scott!

JEFF: I'm going to check to see how much longer I have to wait. This is not right. I told them I had to be taken on time. I called them twice and told them.

HOWARD: Try to relax. Let's find you another picture.

JEFF: I'm going to find out what's going on. (*He exits.*)

HOWARD: He's a nervous little thing, isn't he? (*No one responds.*) I'm sorry I'm disturbing you. I had nothing else to do this afternoon. So I got here early. That's why I'm waiting. That kid made me edgy. Sorry. I'm disturbing you.

GENE: It's all right.

SCOTT: (*To* HOWARD) Do you get chemo?

HOWARD: No, I'm sorry.

SCOTT: (*Sarcastically*) What do you have to be sorry about?

HOWARD: I'm sorry I can't tell you anything about it. You seem worried. I'm sure the nurse will answer all your questions. (*He picks up* JEFF's *magazine.*)

SCOTT: I bet she will. (*To* GENE) You're going to be late getting back to the office.

GENE: It's okay. I told them what I was doing.

SCOTT: You told them what I was coming here for?

GENE: Of course. What's the secret?

SCOTT: Goddamn it, Gene. I don't want people to know about my treatment.

GENE: Why not?

SCOTT: Because it's my treatment.

GENE: People want to know what's going on with you.

SCOTT: Why? They're not my close friends.

GENE: They're mine. And I need their support.

SCOTT: Your office friends are arrogant bastards.

GENE: You don't like anybody these days.

HOWARD: (*Putting down the magazine*) I wish I had my book with me. I forgot it at home. I'm reading *Middlemarch*. It's fat and glorious. I only read thick books now. I figure nothing bad can happen to you when you're in the middle of a long, long story. It's been working so far.

(JEFF *enters.*)

JEFF: They're going to start taking people in a minute. (*Referring to* SCOTT) They said you're ahead of me.

SCOTT: You can go first if you want.

JEFF: (*Suddenly*) I have to go. I've waited too long. You know, the pay phone is broken. I have to call home or get home. I better go.

HOWARD: Do you think you should?

JEFF: I have to. I told them they had to take me on time today. I told them.

HOWARD: What's the matter?

JEFF: I have to go. Maybe I'll see you next week. (*He exits.*)

GENE: That guy is setting himself up for a coronary.

HOWARD: I wonder how he's going to get home? Should somebody have gone with him?

GENE: Is he a friend?

HOWARD: No. I just met him today.

(*They are interrupted by a voice coming from the public address system.*)

VOICE: Mister Donnelly. Mister Donnelly, please report to room 4. Room 4.

SCOTT: (*Frightened*) I don't want to go!

GENE: Come on, you have to.

HOWARD: I should have helped him home.

VOICE: Mister Donnelly...room 4. Room 4.

SCOTT: I don't want to go!

(*Blackout*)

Scene Two

(*Another Tuesday*)

(JEFF *is alone in the room. He is staring intently at the postcard he is holding. After a few seconds,* HOWARD *enters. He has been shopping. He is clutching several packages and his copy of* Middlemarch.)

HOWARD: Well, hello. What's the picture this week?

JEFF: It's a painting. By Monet. (*Showing* HOWARD *the postcard*) Of his gardens at Giverny. Wouldn't you love to live in this painting?

HOWARD: Never. The pollen would kill me.

JEFF: That's too bad.

HOWARD: Did you get home all right last week?

JEFF: Yes, thank you. They promised they would take me exactly on time this week.

HOWARD: That's good.

JEFF: On Tuesday's I'm on a tight schedule. I have banking to do. I have to go to social services, get shopping done, come here. I can't afford to waste any time.

HOWARD: You sound busy.

JEFF: I don't like being away from my apartment too long. My lover's there. He's sick. Quite sick. I don't like being away from him. These are precious moments, right?

HOWARD: Right.

JEFF: At this point, he only likes me to take care of him. When he's up to it, sometimes we sit together, hold hands, and listen to music. Or maybe watch a movie on the V C R. Our friends chipped in and bought us one. That was good of them, wasn't it?

HOWARD: Yes.

JEFF: We know lovely people. On days when we both have a resurgence of energy, I play for him. He loves that. I used to be a concert pianist.

HOWARD: What a comfort your music must be.

JEFF: I love the very idea of it. Selecting sounds from the universe. Giving them an order. They apologized for last week. Did I tell you they said they might even take me early?

HOWARD: Great.

JEFF: You've been shopping.

HOWARD: I've been depressed. This morning I was paying bills. I used to make a good income, but now even the telephone bill terrifies me.

JEFF: May I ask what you do?

HOWARD: Right now, I'm bartending a few days a week. Off the books. But I used to be a therapist. Both occupations are frighteningly similar. All you have to do is listen, and people will throw money at you.

JEFF: Did you have fun shopping?

HOWARD: I should have done this a few weeks ago. I'm sure those T-cells of mine are dropping through economic fear. I've been pinching pennies for too many months now. So this morning I gave myself a good talking to and then went out on a spree. I just handed the cashiers my credit card and never peeked at the bills. I figured I'll take a look while I'm in session with Louise. Let her deal with it.

JEFF: Let anybody else deal with it.

HOWARD: Wouldn't it be fabulous if you could wrap AIDS and all that comes with it in a box and hand it over to a friend? Just for a day. How about a week? A month?

JEFF: That would be mean.

HOWARD: I mean temporarily. It would give us a break. They would learn something. Know what it's really like. It would be fabulous. Maybe for a year.

(*They are interrupted by a voice coming from the public address system.*)

VOICE: Mister Ferris. Mister Ferris, please report to room 4. Room 4.

JEFF: See, they kept their word. They're taking me early.

HOWARD: So it's Ferris.

JEFF: Yes. Jeff Ferris.

HOWARD: Howard Salvo.

JEFF: Good meeting you. I've got to run. I don't want to keep them waiting. (*He begins to leave.*)

HOWARD: (*Calling after him*) When you gave concerts, did you specialize in anything?

JEFF: Yes. The French. I was known for my French repertoire.

(*Blackout*)

Scene Three

(Another Tuesday)

(When the lights come up, SCOTT *and* GENE *are the only men in the room. They are in the middle of an argument.)*

GENE: It was four-thirty. Four-thirty in the morning. An ACT-UP meeting my ass.

SCOTT: After the meeting, some of the guys took me out for a beer.

GENE: A beer? You smelled like a brewery. What kind of jerks do you hang out with? Don't they know you're sick?

SCOTT: They know.

GENE: Then they're fools.

SCOTT: Why don't you leave and go to work.

GENE: You shouldn't be drinking.

SCOTT: Gene, two beers.

GENE: You should be in bed early.

SCOTT: I had fun last night.

GENE: Doing what?

SCOTT: Go! Just leave!

GENE: You don't know how to take care of yourself. That's always been your problem.

SCOTT: What do you mean by that?

GENE: Just that I want you taking better care of yourself.

*(*HOWARD *enters carrying a package and his* Middlemarch.*)*

HOWARD: Well, how are my sweet ones?

SCOTT: We're not your sweet ones.

HOWARD: Missy is sour today.

SCOTT: God, what a tired queen.

HOWARD: I hope your chemo makes you bald.

SCOTT: Take that back!

HOWARD: Twirl on your own finger!

SCOTT: Take it back!

HOWARD: Bald!

(SCOTT *leaps at* HOWARD *and grabs him by his shirt.*)

GENE: (*Trying to separate the men*) Stop it!

SCOTT: (*Not letting go*) I'll clean this room with you if you don't take it back.

HOWARD: Little tough boys bore me. Move those hands.

SCOTT: Take it back. (*Beginning to break down*) Please. Please, take it back. (*He releases* HOWARD. *Breaking down*) Please.

HOWARD: (*Trying to calm* SCOTT *down*) I'm sorry. Really. I am.

SCOTT: Please.

HOWARD: I take it back.

(SCOTT *is sobbing.* HOWARD *takes him into his arms.*)

HOWARD: I take it back.

(*Blackout*)

Scene Four

(Another Tuesday)

*(*HOWARD *is reading his book.* DENISE *is pacing back and forth. She is an attractive black woman who is trying to conceal her nerves.)*

DENISE: You can't smoke here, can you?

HOWARD: No.

DENISE: That's too bad.

HOWARD: I don't think so.

DENISE: *(Suddenly)* You have AIDS don't you?

HOWARD: Why?

DENISE: I want to make sure I'm in the right place.

HOWARD: You're in the right place.

DENISE: Good. What kind of treatment do you get here?

HOWARD: I talk to a therapist.

DENISE: I like therapy. I'm in a group. It's a lot of fun.

HOWARD: Fun?

DENISE: All you do is talk and listen. It's fun. People are usually polite. They make you feel good. But I don't take it too seriously. I mean we all have to leave and go home. And these days, that definitely is not fun.

HOWARD: Where do you live?

DENISE: Out on Long Island. I had to take that goddamn train to get here. I've been selected to be in some study. Some experimental drug. My family is all excited. But to tell you the truth, if I had to win something, I would have preferred the lotto or a scholarship to Yale. Experiments make me nervous. My doctor said I should be delighted. But I can't help wondering, why me? Is it because I'm black? When I said that to my doctor, she said I was getting paranoid.

Perhaps. Then she told me that a lot of gay men were going on this drug. I asked her to show me one straight white man who would be participating. Then maybe I would show more enthusiasm.

HOWARD: You're too much.

DENISE: Denise.

HOWARD: Howard.

DENISE: I wish we were meeting somewhere else.

(SCOTT *and* GENE *enter.*)

SCOTT: Not one hair. Not one hair has fallen out.

HOWARD: Terrific.

(HOWARD *and* SCOTT *embrace.*)

SCOTT: I appreciated your call. It helped.

HOWARD: Don't isolate yourself.

GENE: He's not isolated.

HOWARD: (*Purposely leaving* GENE *out of the introductions*) Denise. Scott.

DENISE: Hi.

GENE: Gene.

DENISE: Hi. (*To* SCOTT) You're on the chemotherapy? You look terrific. You don't even look sick? (*To* GENE) What are you here for?

GENE: I'm not sick.

DENISE: Really?

GENE: What do you mean? Do I look sick?

DENISE: I was just wondering what you were doing here?

GENE: (*Indicating* SCOTT) I come with him.

DENISE: Aren't you kind.

GENE: But I'm not sick. As a matter of fact, I'm not even H I V positive. I test negative. Every time.

(SCOTT *starts applauding.*)

GENE: Stop that!

SCOTT: I'm proud of you. You refrained from mentioning that here for over a month. (*To* DENISE *and* HOWARD) Usually it's within an hour of meeting someone new that he makes his announcement.

GENE: That's unfair.

SCOTT: You practically carry a banner.

GENE: I'm leaving.

SCOTT: Fine.

GENE: To treat me like this in front of your friends.

DENISE: I just met him.

GENE: (*Referring to* HOWARD) I meant him.

SCOTT: Gene, go to work.

GENE: Aren't you relieved I'm negative?

SCOTT: Of course. But you advertise it the same way you advertise your condos. You're relentless.

HOWARD: You own condos?

SCOTT: He sells them.

DENISE: So does my sister-in-law. She loves it. Says it's a real cushy job.

GENE: I work hard.

DENISE: I'm sure you do. But she used to teach in a city school.

GENE: May I say something?

HOWARD: No.

GENE: Why not?

HOWARD: Because whenever someone starts a statement like that, they are about to tell you something you don't want to hear.

GENE: I'm going to say it anyway.

HOWARD: I knew you would.

GENE: You people can be pompous and self-righteous. There. I said it.

DENISE: What people does he mean?

HOWARD: Sick people.

GENE: I'm sorry, but I had to say it.

HOWARD: Bravo.

(GENE *walks over to* SCOTT *and awkwardly gives him a kiss.*)

GENE: I'll see you at home. (*He waits for* SCOTT *to respond.*) I said...

SCOTT: I heard you.

(GENE *leaves.*)

SCOTT: He didn't used to be like that.

HOWARD: It's the pressure.

DENISE: It's men. God, I'm glad I'm taking a break from them. (*To* HOWARD) You live with somebody?

HOWARD: I used to.

DENISE: (*To* SCOTT) What you need honey is a vacation from him.

SCOTT: Impossible. At the moment he's supporting me.

DENISE: That's a bitch.

HOWARD: (*To* SCOTT) Aren't you still working?

SCOTT: My employers forced an early retirement on me. I worked at Fairyland.

DENISE: Is that a dance club?

SCOTT: No, it's a pre-school. They told me they didn't want me deteriorating in front of the children's eyes. Forcing concepts on them that they weren't ready for. They said at my kids' ages only bunny rabbits should get sick and die. So I let them buy me off. They told the kids I was going on a trip. They gave me a bon voyage party and kept me on the payroll for six months. Maybe I should have fought them. I miss the kids.

DENISE: Anytime you want, you can take my two.

(They are interrupted by a voice from the public address system.)

VOICE: Mrs McMillan, report to room 3. Mrs McMillan to room 3.

DENISE: They better answer all my questions.

HOWARD: They'll try to rush you, but see to it that they don't.

DENISE: See you later.

HOWARD: Good luck.

(DENISE exits.)

SCOTT: *(After a moment)* How do you keep it together?

HOWARD: Linguini and clam sauce. Any time I want it.

(Blackout)

Scene Five

(Another Tuesday)

(GENE is standing away from SCOTT thumbing through a magazine. SCOTT is seated staring at the door that leads to the treatment center.)

GENE: Maybe we should think about Europe next year.

(SCOTT starts to cry.)

GENE: Oh babe, please don't.

SCOTT: (*Trying to control himself*) I'm okay. I'll be okay.

(GENE *goes over to* SCOTT.)

(*Blackout*)

Scene Six

(*Another Tuesday*)

(HOWARD, SCOTT, *and* GENE *are seated.*)

HOWARD: I'm worried about that guy. The pianist.

SCOTT: Jeff?

HOWARD: I haven't seen him in weeks. I tried calling him, but he's not listed. And they won't give me any information here.

GENE: Confidentiality. You should be glad.

HOWARD: His lover is sick.

SCOTT: I don't think I want to know.

HOWARD: I hope he's all right.

GENE: He said he doesn't want to know.

HOWARD: Maybe they're listening to music.

GENE: Did you hear him?

SCOTT: Gene, chill out.

HOWARD: Sorry. (*To* SCOTT) How are you doing?

SCOTT: (*Cheerfully*) Pretty good.

HOWARD: Great.

SCOTT: How about you?

HOWARD: Getting along.

(*Pause*)

SCOTT: It's a fine day out there, isn't it? So clear.

(Pause)

HOWARD: Do you think he's got somebody to take care of him?

(Blackout)

Scene Seven

(Another Tuesday.)

(HOWARD, DENISE, GENE, *and* SCOTT *are sitting almost totally still listening to* JEFF. *He is in a state of near hysteria.)*

JEFF: ...I kept repeating, over five thousand times a day, "This isn't happening to me. This isn't happening." In one month my entire life...gone. It disappeared. Everything. And where to? Mack's death wasn't what I expected. And what happened afterwards I just wasn't prepared for. "This isn't happening to me." He was home. He slipped...that's the expression people used... slipped into a coma as if by means of a slate of ice. He slipped. I was afraid to be alone. Afraid I was going to do something wrong. Hurt him in some way. Friends stayed with me around the clock. Took shifts. I could tell they were praying for him to die. Some of them had done this before. They knew what to do. They were sad. I know that. It just wasn't that special to them. Not anymore. "It's time," they said. I knew they had said that in some other room. In someone else's home. "This isn't happening to me." Still, I was holding on to him. Didn't want him to die. I couldn't imagine living in a world where Mack wasn't breathing. "This isn't happening to me." I was exhausted when he died. Had been up for three days. Harry was with me. He made a mistake. Instantly he called 911. The police came. Since the apartment wasn't in my name, they told me they would have to seal it up until the official cause of

death was documented and Mack's next of kin arrived.
Mack's brother—Mack never liked him—would be
handing me back our things, my things. "This isn't
happening to me." As they were taking Mack away—
they put him in a bag—Harry was putting some things
together for me in my overnight bag. Everyone was
rushing around as if we were running to catch a plane.
"Mack, we're not taking a plane anywhere. We're not
going on a vacation. This isn't happening to me." Our
friends were in a fury at my being locked out of my
home. That's what they kept talking about all evening.
Not the obvious. Mack was dead. I would never see
him again. "This isn't happening to me." A quick
cremation. I scattered his ashes near the boat pond in
Central Park. A little place where we picnicked. His
brother and mother were furious. They wanted a body.
Lots of ceremonies. But I did what Mack wanted. They
were as much a part of his death and illness as they
were a part of his life. They were no part. They wanted
things. In the apartment, once I was allowed back in,
they kept asking me, "Is this yours?" How does "ours"
get split into "yours or his or mine?" What right did
they have to ask me? "This isn't happening to me."
I didn't want to fight them. I let them have so many
of our things. The truth was—what was I going to do
with a complete household and no home. The landlady
thought she was being so loving by letting me stay one
more month. Nine years in that apartment. I made it
a home. Our home. My home. "This isn't happening
to me." My lover's dead. I'm sick. I don't have much
money. I have to find a place to live. I'm living out of a
suitcase in a friend's living room. Did I tell you, I had
to sell my piano?

(Blackout)

Scene Eight

(Another Tuesday)

*(*HOWARD *and* GENE *are seated on opposite sides of the room.)*

GENE: *(After a moment)* I've joined a support group for guys who have lovers with H I V.

HOWARD: *(Barely paying attention)* Good.

GENE: We've started a bowling league.

HOWARD: *(Sarcastically)* You guys really know how to get down and dirty.

GENE: You can't stand me.

HOWARD: *(Friendly)* You're right. And it's so upsetting to me. You can be rude, but God, I live in New York. I should be used to it. I spent my entire last session with my therapist only talking about you.

GENE: I wish you hadn't.

HOWARD: Oh, I had to. I have to get to the bottom of this. I must say I was disappointed in Louise's first analysis. She jumped to the obvious. That I was attracted to you. Who does she think she's talking to? Of course, I had already thought of that. In fact the other night I even tried getting up a fantasy about you. I tried to picture you undressed.... My sitting next to you.... But I swear, nothing, nothing happened. But don't worry, I'll figure it out.

GENE: I don't care. This is not my problem.

HOWARD: You're absolutely right. I was talking to my friend Willy about you....

GENE: Next you'll be on Oprah....

HOWARD: Relax. Willy is such a hoot. You'd love him. But maybe you wouldn't. He said it was our past lives. That you must have been a real prick to me in one of them. And that it's sort of spilled over into this lifetime. Who were you Gene? Attila the Hun, the Marquis de Sade, Medea....

GENE: She wasn't real.

HOWARD: You're right. Very good. Oh, don't look so worried. Maybe I was the prick.

(SCOTT *enters from the treatment center.*)

GENE: That was quick.

HOWARD: They think they're working on an assembly line in there.

SCOTT: I didn't take my treatment today.

GENE: Why?

SCOTT: I want to go for a bike ride.

GENE: I know what this is about. A few hairs. You lost just a few hairs.

SCOTT: They were mine. (*He exits.*)

GENE: (*After a moment*) He'll be back.

(*Blackout*)

Scene Nine

(*Another Tuesday*)

(HOWARD *is seated.* DENISE *is pacing.*)

DENISE: I want it just like the old days. I want a good old-fashioned public hanging. You know the kind where people would bring their sewing. I don't sew, but maybe I'd file my nails. I'd get there early. Sit right in the front row. He would scream and cry. I know it. I'd be humming while I was filing my fucking nails. I'd even give the bastard a smile when he climbed the platform.

HOWARD: And I'd be sitting right next to you.

DENISE: What would you be doing?

HOWARD: Reading my book. I'd glance up a couple of times. I'd pretend I was bored. That his execution didn't matter that much.

DENISE: We'd act just like he did. Social services, my ass. Social abuse, that's what they should call his department. He was filling out his appointment book while he was talking to me. (*Imitating a man's voice*) "I'm going to have to bring up something that you're avoiding. Have you thought of your children Mrs McMillan? Where will they go when you're not here? It's best not to wait until the last minute for these kinds of things. We better start making plans." We? That scum bag doesn't think I have a brain in my head. What does he think I think about day after day after day? My mother is old. She may go first. What's he think I am? Some dog? Some bitch that has a litter that has to be disposed of? (*In a fury*) He wasn't even looking at me. He was writing things down in his appointment book.

HOWARD: He'd hear us. Talking about a new restaurant we'd be going to as soon as the show was over.

DENISE: (*Breaking down*) He glanced up at me, maybe twice. Like over his glasses. Checking me out. Seeing if the animal had a reaction.

HOWARD: I'd tell you a joke.

DENISE: (*After a moment*) And I'd laugh as I looked at him.

(*Blackout*)

Scene Ten

(Another Tuesday)

(HOWARD *is staring at* SCOTT *who is beaming.*)

HOWARD: Give me some.

SCOTT: What?

HOWARD: Whatever it is you are on. You look euphoric.

SCOTT: Not quite. Almost. Where's our little friend?

HOWARD: Jeff? He's moved away. Down to Florida. His mother has taken him in. He said he would write. I hope he does.

SCOTT: I hope she's good to him.

HOWARD: I'm sure she will be. She's a piano teacher.

SCOTT: Good. They'll have something to talk about. What time is your appointment?

HOWARD: In a few minutes.

SCOTT: Do you want me to wait around for you? And then maybe we could do dinner—cheap of course.

HOWARD: Of course.

SCOTT: ...and maybe a movie or something.

HOWARD: That would be lovely.

SCOTT: Great.

HOWARD: I don't believe it. This is fabulous. I have a date.

SCOTT: (*Suddenly worried*) It's not a date. We're just going to be like buddies—hanging out.

HOWARD: (*Nervously*) I know, I know.

SCOTT: No date.

HOWARD: Right. We're just friends. Spending some time together.

SCOTT: I just didn't want you to expect something that's not going to happen.

HOWARD: You *are* feeling good.

SCOTT: What do you mean?

HOWARD: You instantly jumped to the conclusion I was after your ass.

SCOTT: But you said date....

HOWARD: Don't worry. You'll be safe with me.

SCOTT: Let's just forget it.

HOWARD: No, please. I'd love to go out with you. But not on a date. Be assured, I'm not going to think of it as a date.

SCOTT: Am I acting like a slime ball?

HOWARD: (*After a moment*) No.

SCOTT: It's just that I never imagined I'd be feeling like this again. Alive. Almost—do I dare say it—hot.

HOWARD: Somebody must have had an awfully good time last night.

SCOTT: No. It's just that I'm going to be free from all this. Free, Howard. Forever more free.

HOWARD: Then what are you doing here? I thought you had come back.

SCOTT: I'm getting my records.

HOWARD: Please, please don't do this.

SCOTT: My Tuesdays are going to be spent in a more pleasant place. Screw their charts. Screw the number they've turned me into. Screw their claim over this body. It's mine again.

HOWARD: (*Worried*) Scott, this is the only help there is for us.

SCOTT: I don't believe their medicines are going to make me any better. I don't believe their drugs will retard my virus.

HOWARD: But they do.

SCOTT: In my soul I don't believe it.

HOWARD: What the hell are you going to do? Get a crystal and start chanting?

SCOTT: Maybe that too. I'm going on a totally holistic trip. Under a doctor's supervision. I'm blowing this joint.

HOWARD: You're playing with your life.

SCOTT: And you're not? You've been brainwashed. I'm going a different way that's all.

HOWARD: Oh Jesus, I'm scared for you.

SCOTT: For the first time in ages I'm not.

(*Blackout*)

Scene Eleven

(*Another Tuesday*)

(HOWARD *and* DENISE *are seated. Both are eating a piece of cake and seem to be enjoying it.*)

DENISE: God, it's good. Are you sure you didn't buy this?

HOWARD: Made it from scratch. I'm totally talented.

DENISE: Will you marry me?

HOWARD: Are you neat?

DENISE: Forget it. Listen darling, can I ask you a question?

HOWARD: Shoot.

DENISE: Have you had any intimacy lately?

HOWARD: A friend came over to dinner the other night, and I couldn't believe how close we got. We talked and talked....

DENISE: And then?

HOWARD: That's all. We just talked.

DENISE: I'm talking about the old push-push.

HOWARD: Oh.

DENISE: Yes, oh. Well?

HOWARD: No.

DENISE: Don't you want to?

HOWARD: Sometimes. I guess so.

DENISE: Then why aren't you getting anything?

HOWARD: You sound like my therapist.

DENISE: I'm making you nervous. I'm sorry. I just thought you were all liberated...

HOWARD: I am.

DENISE: ...and being a shrink yourself you were able to talk easily about all sorts of things.

HOWARD: I can.

DENISE: You are lying. You are as uptight as any of us.

HOWARD: I am not. It's just that I'm ambivalent right now.

DENISE: Same as being uptight. Do you feel unclean?

HOWARD: Sometimes...yes.

DENISE: That's how I usually feel. That was until the other night. Two of my girlfriends took me out. They're in the drug program with me. I usually say no to them, but this time I felt—why not. They act superior sometimes. They don't have AIDS. But generally they're nice. What a party crowd we make. We don't do drugs or drink. But we chain-smoked our cigarettes and tried to act "with it". The music was loud. I was about to get a headache when this guy asked me to dance. It was the first time in over two years that a man had his arms around me. That dance depressed the hell out of me.

HOWARD: Why? Didn't you like the song?

DENISE: I felt like an old lady. There could be no follow up to the dance. Not even a dream of one.

HOWARD: Of course there could be.

DENISE: Get real girl. What was I supposed to say? "Let's get to know each other? Should we go to a movie next week? How about dinner...."

HOWARD: (*Interrupting her*) Yes.

DENISE: "...But don't get too interested in me, because I have.... Should I give you three guesses? Let's just say it begins with an A, and it's not asthma."

HOWARD: What happened?

DENISE: Nothing. I pretended I was from out of town. I feel like I'm from the moon.

HOWARD: We know how to be safe. We can't stop living.

DENISE: It's fucked.

HOWARD: (*After a moment*) We have to do something.

DENISE: Well Einstein, think on it. When you get a vision, give me a call. You wouldn't consider going straight, would you?

HOWARD: That's your second proposition tonight.

DENISE: I'm getting desperate.

HOWARD: Thanks a lot. Maybe you should take out an ad.

DENISE: Where? In some porno rag?

HOWARD: No. In a classier publication. Something like *The New York Review of Books*.

DENISE: You need a CAT scan. The virus has hit your brain.

HOWARD: You have a pen?

DENISE: Yes.

HOWARD: Okay. As fast as you can, write an ad for yourself. I'll write one for you. We'll see what we come up with.

DENISE: I wonder how long you have after the virus enters your brain.

HOWARD: Come on.

(HOWARD *starts writing on the back cover of his book.* DENISE *picks up a magazine to write on.*)

HOWARD: And make sure you give it a bit of spark.

DENISE: Of course. "Poor Black Diseased Woman with two children..." Won't that send them beating down my door.

HOWARD: That's not all you are. You're also attractive, witty....

DENISE: Okay. "Poor Witty Diseased Black...."

HOWARD: You are not diseased...so to speak.

DENISE: So to speak.

(GENE *enters.*)

GENE: Hi guys.

HOWARD: Is Scott coming back?

GENE: Howard, you have to talk to him.

(Although HOWARD *and* DENISE *seem to be giving* GENE *their attention, they still continue, at various moments, working on their ads.)*

HOWARD: How is he?

GENE: Fine. For the time being.

DENISE: Good.

GENE: No, not good. With all this seaweed nonsense, he's endangering his life. He won't listen to me. But he respects you Howard. Why don't you give it a try?

HOWARD: This is not my business.

GENE: But you've become his friend.

HOWARD: And I'd like to stay that way.

GENE: Your friend is standing on a train track and a train is speeding towards him. You're not going to suggest that he might get the hell out of its way?

HOWARD: This is different.

GENE: Do you believe in what he's doing?

HOWARD: No. But he does.

GENE: Don't give me this new age nonsense.

HOWARD: *(To* DENISE*)* Do you like books?

DENISE: Who's got time to read?

HOWARD: Do you like them?

DENISE: I guess so.

GENE: What are you people doing?

DENISE: We're writing an advertisement for me so I can get a boyfriend. You got any ideas?

GENE: You people are no longer playing with a full deck.

DENISE: This is a hell of a lot more fun than thinking about the new drug they're going to shoot me up with today. I think I'm going to say I'm sophisticated. It sounds more high-toned.

GENE: My lover is killing himself....

HOWARD: That's not necessarily true.

GENE: And you guys are in lulu land.

HOWARD: Let go Gene.

GENE: These goddamned cliché phrases. "Let go." I'm not talking about an idea here. I'm talking about a man. My lover. Because of all this wheat-grass shit, he no longer trusts me. Doesn't think I have his best interest at heart. Lumps me in with the government, the medical profession. We can't even sit in front of the television without there being some kind of tension. My home is no longer a pleasant place to be.

HOWARD: (*Not paying attention*) I'm sorry.

GENE: My kitchen now looks like a laboratory. He can't take on a part-time job because of his health. But he spends five hours a day cooking up this slop. Did you know, he has to bleach his vegetables with Clorox?

HOWARD: (*Not paying attention*) I'm sorry.

GENE: We can't even go to a restaurant together anymore. We used to love going to restaurants.

HOWARD: (*Not paying attention*) I'm sorry.

GENE: (*Furiously*) Listen to me goddamn it! (*He grabs the book out of* HOWARD's *hand and rips the page* HOWARD *has been writing on. He is trying not to break down.*) My whole life I dreamed of a having a lover. A partner. A sane, whole one. I wanted a lover with a future. I wanted us to have a future.

HOWARD: (*Meaning it*) I'm sorry. I am.

GENE: Like hell you are.

(GENE *exits.* HOWARD *and* DENISE *watch him leave.*)

DENISE: (*After a moment, looking at the crumbled page from* HOWARD's *book*) What did your ad say?

(*Blackout*)

Scene Twelve

(*Another Tuesday*)

(JEFF *appears excited. On the other side of the room a young man,* RANDY, *sits filling out forms. After a moment,* HOWARD *enters. When he does,* JEFF *jumps up, pulls out a toy horn, blows it and shouts.*)

JEFF: Surprise!

(RANDY *appears shocked by this behavior.*)

HOWARD: I don't believe my eyes.

JEFF: I'm back.

HOWARD: For how long?

JEFF: Forever. Two more weeks in Florida and I would have been up for matricide.

HOWARD: Your mother and you got along that well?

JEFF: Don't get me wrong, I love my mother. She's a decent human being. Brimming with humanity. But my AIDS made her hyperactive. It was like she was on speed. She talked constantly. I fell asleep and woke up to the sound of her voice. She became obsessed with becoming the greatest mother who ever lived. She was out to prove that Jesus got gypped with that light weight mother of his. By the time I arrived she was an expert on AIDS. N Y U Medical Center could use her. She cooked all the time. Special foods for the immune system. My mother can't cook. Never could. Have you ever tried to digest charcoal broiled, burnt, bean curd? Did I ever tell you when we were children, my sister and I had ulcers. Little baby ulcers.

They're back. Only this time they're great big ones.
She developed a routine. She became kind of a positive
thinking Miami Beach Cassandra. Always talking
about how fabulously I was doing. Peppering all talk
with a kind of Walt Disney spirituality. Introducing
me to everyone— "This is my brave, wonderful son.
He has AIDS, you know." By the end of two weeks
we were more famous than Regis and Kathie Lee. I
was beginning to forget my own name. I was just the
son with AIDS. I knew I had had it the night I dreamt
my mother was pureed to death in a juicer. The next
morning she was doing her act in K-Mart. (*Imitating his
mother*) "What's your name honey? Fay Ann. Fay Ann,
this is my son. Do you see the light in his eyes? That's
because he's special. He's been given a special burden,
and he's conquering it. He has AIDS." I lost it. I turned
to her and said, "Mother you have to stop telling that
story up and down the beach. You have to accept
that you're the one with AIDS." The poor woman just
started screaming. It was the first real feeling she had
since I arrived. She screamed all the way home. Even
up the elevator. I told the ladies who were riding with
us that she had just heard Lucille Ball was dead. She
so wanted me out of Miami that she believed the most
stupid lie. I told her that the Academy of Music—
whatever that may be— was giving me a rent free
apartment in New York. She said she would visit. In a
few months.

HOWARD: Where are you staying?

JEFF: With a friend. I told him it's only for a week. He
thinks I'm just visiting from Miami. I don't want to
freak him out.

HOWARD: Jeff, you have no money. What are you going
to do?

JEFF: I don't know. I'm just happy to be out of Miami. I never thought I would do anything like that. Just pack up and leave. I'm getting daring.

RANDY: (*Under his breath*) Fool.

JEFF: What?

RANDY: Go home.

JEFF: This is my home.

HOWARD: Honey, now this might not happen, but suppose you get sick.

JEFF: There's no reason for anyone to worry, because I have health insurance. I have no money. But I do have health insurance.

RANDY: (*Nervously*) I'm trying to fill out these forms. Will you please keep it down?

JEFF: Sorry.

HOWARD: (*To* RANDY) This is a public space. People can talk.

RANDY: Well, I just don't feel like listening to other people's problems at the moment. Okay?

HOWARD: Then go somewhere else. Try another planet.

RANDY: But I may need their help.

HOWARD: Then you're just going to have to concentrate harder.

JEFF: Maybe we should continue this conversation over coffee.

HOWARD: No, we'll have it now.

JEFF: Later. After you're finished with Louise.

HOWARD: I'm not seeing her today.

JEFF: Then why are you here? Who are you seeing?

HOWARD: Doctor Willis.

JEFF: But he's the cancer doctor.

HOWARD: A couple of spots. That's all.

JEFF: Not K S too.

HOWARD: Please don't get upset.

JEFF: (*Obviously shaken*) Can I hold you?

HOWARD: I'm all right.

RANDY: They expect me to fill out their damn forms with the two of you in the room. Well, the hell with them. I shouldn't be here. I'm not like you guys. I'm not going to make a career out of this disease.

HOWARD: (*To* RANDY) Good for you.

JEFF: (*To* HOWARD) How long have you had K S?

RANDY: I'm getting out of here.

HOWARD: (*To* RANDY) Do you need help with the forms?

RANDY: Why do they need to know some of these things?

JEFF: Howard, I just asked you a question.

HOWARD: (*To* RANDY) What things?

RANDY: (*Ripping the forms up and giving them to* HOWARD) If they come looking for me, tell them here are their forms.

HOWARD: (*To* RANDY) Oh, sit down.

RANDY: And tell them they can shove every one of their questions. (*He exits.*)

HOWARD: Denial.

JEFF: What about yours?

HOWARD: And yours?

JEFF: That you can't lay on me.

HOWARD: You have no place to live.

JEFF: How long have you had K S?

HOWARD: Over a month. (*Strongly*) I don't want to talk about that right now.

JEFF: Fine. (*After a moment*) And we're not going to talk about my living situation.

HOWARD: Fine.

JEFF: So what are we going to talk about?

HOWARD: (*After a moment*) What are you doing tonight?

JEFF: Nothing.

HOWARD: How about a movie?

JEFF: I'm watching money.

HOWARD: My treat.

JEFF: Are you sure?

HOWARD: (*Jokingly*) But no popcorn.

JEFF: Cheap.

HOWARD: What should we see?

JEFF: Oh...something new...

HOWARD: And terrible...

JEFF: And funny...

HOWARD: With young people.

JEFF: Something where the people look forward to the future.

HOWARD: Something that has nothing to do with life.

(*Blackout*)

Scene Thirteen

(Another Tuesday)

(JEFF *is seated. He has a suitcase near him.* HOWARD *seems agitated.)*

HOWARD: You can't keep living like this Jeff. Permanent plans have to be made.

JEFF: That seems to be impossible.

HOWARD: You're much too passive.

JEFF: No, I'm not. I left Miami.

HOWARD: For what? To be out on the streets?

JEFF: Things have a way of turning up.

HOWARD: Oh, for Chrissake.

JEFF: Look, Scott said he had a place for me. For a whole month.

HOWARD: Where is this place?

JEFF: I don't know.

HOWARD: Are you going to be living with somebody?

JEFF: I don't know.

HOWARD: I don't believe you.

JEFF: *(On the verge of tears)* What am I supposed to do? Please stop this.

HOWARD: I want you to wake up.

JEFF: I'm awake Howard. I'm handling all that I can. I got through the last hour. I'm getting through this one.

HOWARD: There's something wrong with you.

JEFF: They tell me I have AIDS. *(He laughs.)*

HOWARD: How many social service agencies do you have working on your case?

JEFF: *(Yelling)* Shut up!

HOWARD: I'm glad to see you yelling.

JEFF: But I'm not.

HOWARD: However, I shouldn't be the object of your rage.

JEFF: (*Imitating Bette Davis*) "But you are Howard. You are." Let's change the subject.

HOWARD: To what?

JEFF: (*After a moment*) Who do you think Cher's next husband or steady will be?

HOWARD: You're impossible.

JEFF: Or do you think she'll play the field and keep people guessing?

HOWARD: We're talking about your life.

JEFF: And I'm trying to get through the next hour.

HOWARD: And I'm trying to be a friend.

(SCOTT *enters.*)

JEFF: Then leave me alone.

SCOTT: What's going on guys? (*Jokingly*) Did Howard make a pass?

HOWARD: We were having a dispute.

JEFF: About Cher's next beau.

SCOTT: Really?

JEFF: Really.

SCOTT: Whatever gets you off. Jeffrey, wait till you see the place I've got for you.

JEFF: Yes.

SCOTT: With a room of your own. Rent free. For six, count them, six weeks.

JEFF: Amazing.

SCOTT: It's a small two bedroom, but real cozy.

JEFF: Is anybody else going to be living there?

SCOTT: Yes.

JEFF: Who?

SCOTT: Me.

HOWARD: Oh, for Chrissake.

JEFF: What happened?

SCOTT: He won't let me live the way I want to live. He criticizes everything I'm doing. (*Imitating* GENE) "Do you want to die? Is that why you're not going to your doctor? Do you want to die?" I can't take it anymore.

HOWARD: You've got to talk to him. Reach some sort of compromise.

SCOTT: It's impossible. It has nothing to do with the holistic stuff I'm doing. When that man looks at me, all he sees is a corpse. I'm not that.

HOWARD: So what are you going to do?

SCOTT: This friend of mine is going to be out of town for six weeks, and he's giving me his place.

HOWARD: After that?

SCOTT: I don't know.

HOWARD: You two can't afford "I don't knows" anymore.

SCOTT: Listen Howard, I'm alive, and while I am I want as much freedom as I can handle. I can't kiss ass and turn over my treatment to somebody for a roof over my head.

HOWARD: That roof is worth a lot.

SCOTT: Not my life.

JEFF: Where's the apartment?

SCOTT: In Chelsea. It faces a courtyard. Gets tons of sun.

JEFF: Does my room have a window?

SCOTT: Yes. A large one.

JEFF: That's good.

HOWARD: It's terrific. In six weeks you can open it and jump out.

(JEFF *laughs.*)

SCOTT: Lighten up Howard.

(*Blackout*)

Scene Fourteen

(*Another Tuesday*)

(JEFF *is thumbing through a magazine.* HOWARD, *appearing nervous, is writing a letter.*)

HOWARD: Damn! It's just not coming out right.

JEFF: What?

HOWARD: My letter.

JEFF: Not another one to the President.

HOWARD: No, to my sister.

JEFF: You have a sister?

HOWARD: Is there anything wrong with that?

JEFF: You never mentioned her.

HOWARD: Didn't I?

JEFF: Therapists are so secretive. They just love dragging stories out of everybody, but they act like it's a major intrusion if you ask them what they had for lunch.

HOWARD: A stuffed pepper.

JEFF: Are you and your sister close?

HOWARD: Used to be. It's our family reunion next weekend. There's going to be party.

JEFF: Will it be fun?

HOWARD: I can't go.

JEFF: Why not?

HOWARD: Because I don't want to. And this letter's all wrong. Would you listen?

JEFF: Of course.

HOWARD: "Dear Janet, So sorry this note has taken so long..." I wrote that "so sorry" part because that's how our Mom starts all her correspondence. Even her Visa bills. Anyway... "So sorry this note has taken so long. I will not be coming to the family reunion. You see, I'm redecorating my bathroom this weekend, and I'm in a conflict as to what color the shower curtain should be."

JEFF: Howard, what the hell is going on?

HOWARD: ..."I know you understand why I can't make it to this place you call home. Because wasn't that your same predicament the week that my Greg died? Oh Howie," you wrote.... "So sorry" ...you actually used Mom's expression.... "But they just started the construction on our kitchen.... Now, after the funeral, come home and I'll take care of you." (*To* JEFF) I haven't been able to talk to her for a year. And now, all I can do is quote her own letter. (*Tearing up the letter*) I can't send this. It's humiliating. Too fucking needy. (*Breaking down*) But not one cousin showed up.

JEFF: (*Going to* HOWARD) It's all right Howard.

HOWARD: (*Furiously*) What the hell is all right?

(*Blackout*)

Scene Fifteen

(*Another Tuesday*)

(DENISE *is pacing.* JEFF *is reading a magazine.*)

JEFF: (*After a moment*) Is anything wrong?

DENISE: I don't want to be here today.

JEFF: I don't either.

DENISE: Is it interesting?

JEFF: What?

DENISE: What you're reading.

JEFF: It's about the renovation of castles. It's the latest thing the European yuppies are buying.

DENISE: So...how's it going?

JEFF: I don't think I'd buy one. Too damp.

DENISE: I mean with you.

JEFF: Great. I just wish it would stop raining.

(HOWARD, *who is walking slowly, enters.*)

HOWARD: So that's what's bothering you these days.

JEFF: Say "hello" before you start in on me.

HOWARD: Hello. (*To* DENISE) And hello stranger. Where'd you disappear to?

DENISE: Scranton.

HOWARD: The one in Pennsylvania?

DENISE: I pray to God there isn't another one.

HOWARD: Were you there on vacation?

DENISE: I'm not tasteless.

HOWARD: You look great.

DENISE: I'm okay. Yes. I think I'm doing okay. I took my kids there.

HOWARD: Why?

DENISE: (*After a moment*) They've moved in with my sister and her husband.

HOWARD: Oh God, no.

DENISE: Yes. But I'm okay. I should be grateful. Now, I know where my kids are going to be. My sister—Colleen—is very loving. So is her husband. They have a baby of their own. Now, they'll be a family of five.

(HOWARD *starts to cry.*)

DENISE: Howard, don't cry, please. I'm okay. We decided it was best for my children to do this now, while I'm doing well. This way, I can go down there—once a month if I want—to see how they're adjusting. I can still be a part of their lives. Howard, don't cry. It doesn't help. Look I've brought you a coffee mug. It says, "Scranton, PA". Classy, isn't it? I took a bus back. That's how you get back from Scranton. You take a bus. The man next to me wanted to chat. Wanted to get to know me. "You're not very friendly are you?" That's what he said. He said it twice. I just stared out the window. Listening to him furiously turning the pages of his magazine. Thousands of people have taken bus rides like mine. Coming from their doctors after they find out. Coming from their families after they've told them. Staring out of windows wanting it to be yesterday. My little one—my boy—when I kissed him good-bye, he immediately left my arms and went and sat in front of the T V. What do you think that poor boy was thinking? My daughter—she acts all grown-up—gave me a big hug and said, "Everything is going to be fine." Sure darling. Sure. They've seen too much already in their baby lives. I hope some day they're happy. Don't cry Howard. It doesn't help.

HOWARD: Again and again. It happens again and again.

JEFF: (*Jumping up*) Howard!

HOWARD: (*Yelling*) When will this stop?!?

JEFF: (*Opening the door to the treatment center*) Get somebody!

DENISE: (*In her own world*) Will they ever be happy?

HOWARD: (*Yelling*) How much more can we take?!? How much more?!?

(HOWARD *lets out a scream.* DENISE *remains seated.* JEFF *remains frozen.*)

(*Blackout*)

Scene Sixteen

(*Another Tuesday*)

(HOWARD *is asleep on the floor.* JEFF *is watching him.*)

JEFF: (*After a moment*) Howard...they called you.

HOWARD: (*Waking up. After a moment*) I was dreaming. (*He struggles to get up.*)

(*Blackout*)

Scene Seventeen

(*Another Tuesday*)

(HOWARD *appears to be engrossed in his book.* JEFF *is watching him.*)

JEFF: Is it good?

HOWARD: *War and Peace.*

JEFF: That should keep you going for a year.

HOWARD: These days I can lick a book like this in a week.

JEFF: You've been that social?

HOWARD: How's Scott?

JEFF: Good. He's fun to live with. He sings. Like around the house. It puts you in a good mood.

HOWARD: When you have to move, do you know where you're going yet?

JEFF: I'm working on it.

HOWARD: What about Scott?

JEFF: He's working on it.

HOWARD: I guess that's good.

JEFF: I wish you'd drop by and visit us.

HOWARD: I don't think so.

JEFF: Why not?

(GENE *enters.*)

GENE: (*Tentatively*) Hi guys.

JEFF: Hello. What brings you here?

GENE: Howard left a message. Said he had to see me. That it was urgent.

HOWARD: I'd like to talk.

GENE: Yes.

HOWARD: Over dinner soon.

GENE: (*Awkwardly*) Oh. Well, I'm taking off for a while. A vacation.

HOWARD: Okay. When you get back.

GENE: I'm not sure when that will be. I'll give you a call. I guess I'll be seeing you guys.

HOWARD: Wait! Gene...do...do you miss Scott?

GENE: (*Embarrassed*) That's not your business.

HOWARD: I'm worried about him.

GENE: I try not to.

HOWARD: You care for him, don't you?

GENE: You're embarrassing me.

HOWARD: I know you do. So you've got to take him back.

JEFF: Howard!

GENE: It's over.

HOWARD: Then be a friend. Love him as a friend.

JEFF: (*To* HOWARD) Stop it! Have some pride.

HOWARD: Screw it!

GENE: I've got to get back to the office.

HOWARD: (*Grabbing* GENE's *arm*) The office? What the fuck you talking about?

JEFF: Howard, don't do this.

GENE: (*To* HOWARD) Let go.

HOWARD: (*Holding tight*) Someone you once loved is sick. Has no money. And in a few weeks will have no place to live.

GENE: (*Shoving* HOWARD *away from him*) I can't think about it anymore.

HOWARD: You have to.

GENE: No! No, I don't. Right now, I can't. I've had enough.

HOWARD: (*Begging*) What about Scott?

GENE: I'm not Scott, and I'm not you. The last two years have been a nightmare. But there's a way out for me, and I'm taking it.

HOWARD: (*Pleading*) What about us? People have to help, don't they? You have to help.

JEFF: Shut up Howard!

GENE: All I have is one life. I want some pleasure.

HOWARD: (*Desperately*) But what about us?

GENE: I pray for you.

(HOWARD *hauls off and slaps* GENE *across the face.* GENE *just stands there.*)

JEFF: (*To* GENE) Get out of here.

GENE: I'll still pray.

JEFF: Go!

(GENE *backs out of the room.*)

HOWARD: Look at me. I'm going crazy. I am. We all are. Every single damn one of us.

(*Blackout*)

Scene Eighteen

(*Another Tuesday*)

(DENISE *is alone. She looks around and seems uncomfortable. A voice comes over the public address system.*)

VOICE: Dennis McMillian report to room 3. Dennis McMillian to room 3.

DENISE: (*After a moment. Softly, almost crying*) It's Denise. Denise. (*She slowly gets up and heads for the treatment center.*)

(*Blackout*)

Scene Nineteen

(Two weeks later)

(JEFF is seated next to HOWARD. HOWARD appears dazed. He has a book in his lap.)

JEFF: You were home. I know you were there.

HOWARD: I probably went out for milk.

JEFF: You were in there. You don't even answer your phone.

HOWARD: I'm just going through a hermit phase. That's all.

JEFF: Why don't you want to be with your friends?

HOWARD: Jeff, lay off, please. Let me get back to my book.

JEFF: Look at me Howard.

HOWARD: No, I can't. I love you Jeff. I love Denise. But I don't want to be with you now. I don't want to think about Denise and her children. I'm like Gene. I don't want to think about you. Your lover. All my dead friends. I just want to read my book.

JEFF: What about you? What kind of thought are you giving yourself? Aren't you sad at what's happening to you? I am. Don't you want to tell me?

HOWARD: Tell you what?

JEFF: That you're getting weaker. That you're losing weight. That you're sleeping all the time. That you're having trouble walking.

HOWARD: Please let me read my book.

JEFF: Talk to me.

HOWARD: Why don't we just forget it.

JEFF: Because we can't. Come on...please...talk to me.

HOWARD: (*After a moment*) Last night...

JEFF: Yes...

HOWARD: ...when I came out of the bathroom, I didn't know where I was. I stood there in my apartment, among my things, and I didn't know where I was.

JEFF: (*Lovingly*) Now, say it. Please.

HOWARD: What?

JEFF: You know.

HOWARD: I'm...

JEFF: Yes.

HOWARD: Afraid. I'm so afraid. (*He begins to cry.*)

JEFF: Don't do this alone.

HOWARD: I don't know how long I stood there. Shaking and wondering where I was.

JEFF: You don't need to do this alone. I'm a terrific nurse.

HOWARD: I can't ask you. You've done it already. I can't ask you to do it again.

JEFF: I'd do it again and again and again if it would help.

HOWARD: You'd come live with me?

JEFF: I'm practically homeless.

HOWARD: Are you neat?

JEFF: I have no idea what a dust ball looks like.

HOWARD: You've got yourself a roommate.

(*JEFF takes* HOWARD *in his arms.*)

(*Blackout*)

Scene Twenty

(Two weeks later)

(SCOTT *and* JEFF *are listening to* DENISE.)

DENISE: The kids are doing okay. Teddy has made a good friend so he's busy and happy. Jeff—you'll appreciate this—Michelle is taking piano lessons and loving it. It was a crazy week-end. My sister and I cooked and drank gallons of coffee. The only problem is Bill, my brother-in-law. He's a beautiful human being—don't get me wrong. This is awful, but I've got to say it. He's the most boring person I've ever met. After dinner one night he was talking a blue streak. I sat there trying to listen, but I fell right to sleep. Had a good doze. The poor guy was embarrassed. I said—this is the worse—that people with AIDS fall asleep constantly. He believed me thank God. Colleen is so vibrant. What could she see in him?

SCOTT: Maybe he's great sex.

DENISE: I doubt it. If I have insomnia now, I picture him talking to me and within minutes I'm in never, never land. I hope his personality doesn't rub off on my children.

JEFF: He can't be that bad.

DENISE: He's a beautiful person. I'm grateful to him. I should keep my mouth shut. He's in hardware. Maybe he's the Michelangelo of light fixtures.

SCOTT: Maybe at night, in his basement, he's working on the great American poem.

JEFF: Or the cure for AIDS.

DENISE: You've got it. You guys are so perceptive. Bill doesn't want to see me get too excited. His boring nature is all a disguise. He's going to come up with a cure for AIDS.

(HOWARD, *who is now using a cane, walks in slowly and looks in pain.*)

HOWARD: Somebody better. And soon.

JEFF: You finished?

HOWARD: Yes. Thank you for coming here Scott. You look good.

SCOTT: Still walking around.

HOWARD: How have you been living?

SCOTT: Sponging off a lot of people.

HOWARD: Is that okay?

SCOTT: Not all the time.

(HOWARD *strokes* SCOTT's *face.*)

HOWARD: I'm glad you're here. I need you people today.

SCOTT: Are they going to put you in the hospital buddy?

HOWARD: Not yet.

JEFF: Great. Then let's get out of here.

HOWARD: I have to sit for a minute. What a day. I got stuck with blind Belinda.

JEFF: I'm sorry. How many times did she stick you before she found a vein?

HOWARD: My arm can now be used as a colander.

JEFF: What did Doctor Willis say?

HOWARD: The news is not good. I may refuse to believe him. I'm wasting away. Disintegrating. I'd rather think of it as a process of evaporation. Do you think I'll be in the air like H-2-O?

(DENISE *embraces* HOWARD. JEFF *and* SCOTT *lovingly watch them.*)

HOWARD: You smell good.

DENISE: Thank you.

HOWARD: Don't let go yet. I have blossomed into a sentimental sponge.

JEFF: He's even taken to watching the re-runs of *The Waltons*.

HOWARD: (*Leaving* DENISE's *embrace*) And you promised you'd never tell.

JEFF: I lied.

HOWARD: Denise, do you believe in God?

DENISE: No.

HOWARD: Shit.

DENISE: Did I give the wrong answer?

HOWARD: I was hoping you did. It would have thrown a nice monkey wrench into my atheism.

SCOTT: I believe in God.

HOWARD: You do?

SCOTT: Why are you surprised?

DENISE: What God do you believe in?

SCOTT: There's only one God.

DENISE: He's a Catholic.

SCOTT: Not anymore. But I am a Christian.

JEFF: No!

SCOTT: Yes.

JEFF: I'll be damned.

SCOTT: I can't believe how shocked you people look.

JEFF: It doesn't seem to fit.

SCOTT: With what?

JEFF: With your politics.

SCOTT: That's narrow minded.

JEFF: Sorry. Maybe if you told us you were into some new age philosophy where they read auras and build pyramids we wouldn't be so surprised.

SCOTT: Well, get ready for this one. I go to church.

JEFF: No.

SCOTT: I take communion. I always have, and I always will.

HOWARD: Even before you got sick?

SCOTT: Yes, Howard.

DENISE: Well, I'll be damned.

JEFF: I lived with you. How come I never knew? Why would you keep it a secret?

SCOTT: What secret? On Sundays I told you I'd bring home bagels after church.

JEFF: I thought it was a poor joke.

DENISE: (*To* SCOTT) You believe in heaven?

SCOTT: Yes.

DENISE: Well, I'll be damned.

SCOTT: If I told you people I was a serial killer, you would be less shocked. Come on Jeff, come out of the closet and admit you're religious too.

HOWARD: You?

JEFF: Not religious. Spiritual. There were rare moments, when I was on stage playing, I would enter another world. There has to be something beyond this. Many other worlds.

DENISE: Well, I'll be damned.

HOWARD: I envy you guys.

DENISE: I don't.

HOWARD: (*To* DENISE) Not even a bit.

DENISE: No. I think some of the stories are nice, but if I believed that there was someone in charge and this is what that person had come up with—I'd walk around pissed all the time.

SCOTT: That's not how it works.

DENISE: I have no interest in any of it. It's better for me to focus on this life and get through it as best I can.

HOWARD: Jeff, I don't think I know how to do this?

JEFF: Do what?

HOWARD: Die.

JEFF: (*After a moment, lovingly*) You're not dying yet. When the time comes, I'm sure it's real easy. Let's go home.

HOWARD: I don't want another night falling asleep in front of the T V.

JEFF: Then we won't turn it on.

HOWARD: I'm sounding like a pain in the ass.

DENISE: You sound drugged.

HOWARD: (*Smiling*) Well, I am...a little. I'd love to be sitting on a porch—looking at something green.

JEFF: Now, you're sounding trite. But if you want, I'll read you an Andy Hardy story.

HOWARD: (*Referring to* JEFF) Do you believe the mouth I live with?

SCOTT: I know a place.

HOWARD: What place?

SCOTT: A place where you can sit on a porch and look out on beautiful farm lands.

HOWARD: Scott, you're not going to take my hand, and we're not going to start a meditation.

SCOTT: But I know a place. Upstate. We can all go for a few days. It's owned by two guys I know. Doctors. They only use it on weekends. They're real generous. I know they'll give me the keys. Let's all go.

DENISE: All of us.

SCOTT: Why not?

DENISE: How do we get there?

HOWARD: We rent a car with my credit card. (*Handing his wallet to* JEFF) Here. Jeff, you arrange it.

SCOTT: I'll call my friends.

DENISE: Do I have time to go home and pack?

SCOTT: (*Exiting*) No.

JEFF: Howard, are you sure you want to do this?

HOWARD: Why not? If I croak while you're getting the car, take me to the country anyway.

JEFF: We'll stuff you in the trunk. This way I'll be able to stretch out in the back seat.

(JEFF *kisses* HOWARD *and exits with* SCOTT.)

DENISE: Aren't we something.

(RANDY, *who appeared in Scene Eleven, walks in and sits down nervously.*)

RANDY: Hi.

HOWARD: Hello.

RANDY: Randy.

HOWARD: Howard.

DENISE: Denise.

RANDY: (*To* HOWARD) Do you remember me?

HOWARD: Yes.

RANDY: I'm back.

HOWARD: I'm sorry.

DENISE: I'd better call my mother and tell her we're going on a trip. *(She exits.)*

RANDY: A vacation?

HOWARD: Sort of.

RANDY: I'm handling things better.

HOWARD: That's good.

RANDY: How have you been doing?

HOWARD: Not well today.

RANDY: I'm sorry.

HOWARD: You look good.

RANDY: I'm handling things better.

HOWARD: Attitude is important.

RANDY: That's what they say. *(Nervously)* What's it like coming here every week?

HOWARD: I've made some wonderful friends.

RANDY: But what's it like?

HOWARD: Different for everyone.

RANDY: That's evasive.

HOWARD: What do you want me to tell you?

RANDY: The truth.

HOWARD: No. You want me to lie and tell you that you'll never get like me.

RANDY: No. I want to know. What's it like? Please.

HOWARD: I can't answer that. Maybe you'll never get as weak as I am. Things are changing.

RANDY: Not fast enough. Tell me something. Anything.

HOWARD: Try to stay in charge.

RANDY: I feel lonely. So separate from everyone I know.

HOWARD: You've moved. You now live on the other side of the street. People on our side are forced to think about and look at things most people are blind to. I know you're thinking about death. Well, look at it. And then go about the business of living.

RANDY: You're a kind man.

VOICE: Mister Tompkins, please report to room 4. Mister Tompkins to room 4.

RANDY: (*Not moving*) That's me. I'm so scared.

HOWARD: Of course you are. Why don't I stay here until you're finished with your treatment.

RANDY: Would you come in with me?

HOWARD: Of course.

VOICE: Mister Tompkins, room 4. Room 4.

RANDY: I haven't told anybody yet.

HOWARD: (*Getting up*) You'll feel better after you do.

RANDY: (*Getting up*) You're probably right.

HOWARD: Are you going to be coming on Tuesdays?

RANDY: Yes. Is it a good day?

HOWARD: The best.

RANDY: Will you be here?

HOWARD: Maybe.

(*Blackout*)

END OF PLAY